UNEXPECTED TREASURE

For my husband
DAVID
one of the many who unknowingly
belong to the great company
of the saints of Wales

JUDY ROBLIN

UNEXPECTED TREASURE

More Letters to Kate

ST PAULS

ACKNOWLEDGEMENTS

Special thanks to Benedicta,who shared the journey and worked wonders with the text.

ST PAULS Publishing
187 Battersea Bridge Road, London SW11 3AS, UK
www.stpaulspublishing.com

ISBN 978-0-85439-773-0

A catalogue record is available for this book from the British Library.

Set by Tukan DTP, Stubbington, Fareham, UK
Printed by Intype Libra Limited, Wimbledon, UK

ST PAULS is an activity of the priests and brothers
of the Society of St Paul who proclaim the Gospel
through the media of social communication.

Foreword

So much of our spiritual reading is written by religious – sometimes all the better for that, but not always. *Unexpected Treasure* is written by a laywoman. It starts from a different place. It expresses the experience of God in different terms. Its phrases, images and examples have a particular texture and colour. These are some of the reasons that make it a special gift.

When the graces of the Incarnation are experienced through the domestic life of home-making, family-raising and marriage-maintaining, then the stories will be told against these backgrounds. They will have their own slant, their own unique emphases and emotions. The felt presence of the divine will be experienced in the context of growing youngsters, their emerging independence, the need for constant forgiveness and letting go, the need to stay in love, and the challenges of the mid-life years.

There is a great tenderness in this enduring conversation between two women, a tenderness too often missing from more prescriptive approaches to holiness. Every line in this book of letters is alive with understanding, encouragement, empathy and compassion. The subtle nuances of love in their letters regularly and inevitably flow over into poetry. We remember the preciousness of the exchanges between Martha and Mary, Mary and Elizabeth, Veronica and Jesus, the women near the Cross.

And so, throughout these pages we catch glimpses into the daily realities of a woman's world – the fears and expectations, the worries and disappointments, the relentless, necessary busyness, yet the yearning for depth. Salvation is filtered through the seasons of two women's lives. Redemption is woven into the simple and complex fabric of their daily relationships and environments. Their faith is located and lived in each unfolding moment of the mystery of their being.

Grace and nature, God's love and human love, are quietly held together in these deep and moving exchanges between two loving friends. For them God is everywhere. What is most truly human is most truly divine. Home, indeed, is a holy place. As St Augustine said, "The love with which we love each other is the same love with which God loves us."

Fr Daniel O'Leary

Preface

It was during her student days that Kate first became aware of God touching her life in new and deeper ways. She expressed this in prayer-poems and letters to her godmother Ailsa – whose lessons in reply never failed to encourage, challenge and inspire.

It seems that often we can only fully appreciate the richness and intensity of what we experience long after it has happened. This came home to Kate in mid-life when, during a house-move, she turned up again those letters from Ailsa. Re-reading them, she realised they had lost none of their old power to excite her, and felt they could do the same for others. When she asked her godmother's permission to publish them, to her surprise Ailsa not only agreed, but fetched out a folder of the poems Kate had sent to her so long ago, which she too had kept safe through the intervening years. In this happy way letters and poems were brought together and the little selection *Letters to Kate* was born. For Kate, however, the spiritual searching of her younger days had now been powerfully rekindled, stirring up many new questions that demanded answers. It was natural that she should turn to the same wise and loving friend who had helped her in the past ...

Letters to Kate ends at the point where Kate leaves university for a time of voluntary service, teaching overseas. This fictionalised account of a life-long exploration into God now catches up with her as a married woman with two teenage sons. Again the invitation is to walk alongside and share part of her journey.

Judy Roblin

My dear Kate

Thank you very much for your letter, which moved me just as much as those you used to write as a student. It was just the sort of letter I hoped you might write once *Letters to Kate* had been published.

You say that re-reading those letters and re-membering the student days they invoke has unsettled you, and you feel a great sense of loss and nostalgia for that time of intensity and passion. You still believe in God and His involvement with our world, but it has become more cerebral than heart-felt, and you think about prayer, rather than actually praying. You realise how lucky you are to have a wonderful husband, two lovely children, a teaching job you enjoy and a circle of good friends. Yet you feel unsatisfied, aware of a painful longing you can't articulate, deep down within yourself. "There must be more for someone like me?" you cry.

You will probably wonder why I was so moved by what you wrote. It is because, dear Kate, I can see that your unrest and hunger for more is nothing less than the Holy Spirit at work in you. All our needs and longings are symptoms of a greater need for God. This is so for everyone (even if we don't recognise it) because that is how we are made. In each of us there lies a gaping hole that only God can fill, because that is how He has chosen to 'programme' us. And that deep painfulness you describe is there for the specific purpose of guiding us home. St Augustine famously said, "My heart is restless till it rests in Thee", while Abbot Jerome Hodkinson of Belmont used to say, "All you need is your need." I believe the passion of old that you long for today is still there, Kate, covered over by layers of living but now bubbling up to the surface again. God is still there waiting for you to turn your face to Him. Your tentative thought of returning to Tymawr for a week is surely also the calling of the Holy Spirit. Pete and the boys will manage to survive without you, and may even see it as a bit of an adventure to be self-supporting for a few days!

I do hope you are able to enjoy this wonderful Indian summer – it will make winter so much shorter. David and I spent a whole day on Barafundle beach last week, and with the children back at school it was deserted. So wondrous! Like being on a Greek island! I can hardly believe that Oliver is almost fourteen years old – it seems only yesterday that you were his age.

With great sympathy and always prayer,

Your loving godmother,

Ailsa

Dear Kate,

I was so pleased to receive your beautiful card and to know the plan is in place for you to visit Tymawr at half-term. It's great the family has responded and I expect they may enjoy a bit of male bonding in your absence. Pete is great, isn't he? We are both so lucky in our partners and the way they allow us space to develop in our own way. It's Kahlil Gibran again, isn't it? "Let there be spaces in your togetherness for the winds of heaven to dance between you."

I do understand how you feel when you say it's like starting all over again with prayer and therefore a bit scary. I loved your analogy of jumping in at the deep end when you know you should be able to swim, but can't remember the strokes. Some of us feel like that most of the time! All we can do then is trust the buoyancy of the water and float in whichever direction it takes us. Don't worry about not having been in touch with Tymawr for a long time; your welcome will be all the warmer for that – both from God and from the sisters.

So, my dear, I shall think of you afloat in the ocean that is God and give thanks that our little endeavour together is bearing fruit and being used by Him to draw you further along the way to Himself. It's Pembroke's Michaelmas Fayre next week and the nights are beginning to draw in, but this weather is still wonderful for putting the garden to bed for the winter.

All my love – and prayer,

Ailsa

WELCOME

Welcome

rains round the roofed windows

of the place where we meet;

torrential,

your love showers my whole self

as you rejoice in my coming –

you more glad that I came

even than I am to be here.

Dear Kate,

What a joy to receive your letter from Tymawr
telling how you slipped back so easily and gently
into the rhythm of life there. And thank you for
the beautiful poem; I'm so glad you have carried
this gift into maturity. I wasn't too surprised to
hear that the stresses and expectations fell away
beneath God's gaze. Time spent in His company
has a habit of doing this. You speak of feeling
'held' again in the silence of the chapel, received
and welcomed as if Christ washed the whole of
you and not only your feet. How wonderful! And
to hear within yourself His words, "You are my
beloved" – it's not surprising you wanted to stay
there for ever. Hold gently this knowledge and
treasure it, just as Mary kept things quietly in
her heart, for in the harsh light of day the
challenge can be a great one to continue to
believe we are so much loved by God. Voices tend
to rise up to tell us we cannot possibly be loved
just as we are without deserving it in some way.
It isn't easy to accept that I can do nothing to
make God love me more than He does, just as
nothing I do can make Him love me less than He

does! Treasure and trust your experience, Kate, because it is absolutely real.

I am delighted too that out of all the books in the Tymawr library your most significant memory was reading de Caussade's *Sacrament of the Present Moment* and his prayer of abandonment. I remember how important it was for you when you had left college and were setting off for Africa and the unknown. It is a little book which, once it has touched you, has the habit of coming back to mind and always more vividly than before. That has certainly been my experience. In many ways, Kate, you need no other book as a guide.

Handing our lives over to God is no easy option and the relinquishing of control can take a lifetime of learning, through all that happens to us. It takes so long because we are not puppets but have choice, and our gentle gracious God never forces Himself on anyone. But if we do persevere with the prayer of abandonment ("I abandon myself into your hands; do with me what you will...") He will not let us down, even when we believe that is just what He has done! Meanwhile, my dear fellow-traveller, perhaps we can hold on to the old Spanish proverb which says: "The question is not what is going to become of us, but what we are going to become!"

I do hope the transition from the mountain-top will be gentle for you, Kate, and in your busy weeks leading up to Christmas I shall be praying that your schedule will allow of some time each day to meet with God.

All my love and prayer,

Ailsa

Dearest Kate,

Thank you so much for your marvellous letter. I well understand your sense of loss at leaving Tymawr, even though Pete and the boys gave you such a great welcome back. You say you worry slightly that you feel all the love they heap upon you is not enough, on its own, without God's love for you too. But what an insight that is! Dear Kate, that is how it is for everyone, but consciously felt and articulated by you, fresh from a week with the Beloved. Fortunately this is in fact no competition at all! We are never called on to make a choice between our husbands and children or God. Rather, all genuine love is God-given and precious to our lives. Flowing naturally from and into each other, there is no separation between the different kinds, in the ocean that is God. Just as your relationship with God overflows into the daily details of your family life, so Pete and the boys are part of the pattern of your relationship with God. All is one, and our failure is only that we do not see the reality of what is.

And yet we are human and I understand your present ache. Although your head tells you that God is calling you, right where you are at home, to a deeper relationship with Him, your heart cannot help but feel a sense of loss when leaving Tymawr, a community which has God as its whole raison d'etre. "Which is the real world?" you ask. But the real answer is simply, "All is one."

On another topic, your urge for an inner spring-clean sounds most cathartic! It's brilliant that you are asking yourself, "What do I want to keep in my life?" rather than focusing on what you want to get rid of. You have obviously made an important discovery. What matters most to you are two things: the family and everything involved with that; and the Eucharist – none of the accompanying paraphernalia. You feel that you are financially bound to keep up the teaching job and I understand that. But I was rather surprised that you seemed ready to consider relinquishing it at all, because I always thought you loved teaching so much. Has something changed there to dampen your enthusiasm?

You have shown great courage Kate, in this re-evaluation of your life and the consequent pruning implied. In particular, it isn't easy to say no to people, mostly because of our deep desire to please, which in turn masks a deep-seated fear of rejection. Also, of course, responding to the demands of others makes us feel important and needed and loving. But you know well enough that this doesn't mean we can ever ignore the real needs of others.

So much to reply to in this last letter of yours! Your concern about 'keeping the vision alive' is a natural one and a worry I can identify with. Yet it is one we need not bother ourselves with too much. God is in charge of that too, and it is He who will keep the sense of His presence vivid for you (or not – as is His best wish for you). Your concern can only be to make space in your life to receive Him. And this is precisely the purpose of the spring-cleaning you have begun so instinctively and so well, under the guidance of the Holy Spirit.

My dear Kate, I get just as much from writing to you as a mature woman, as I did when you were young. I recognise the same hunger for God, re-ignited and even more beautiful! And yes, of course I am happy to continue the exchange as in the past, though this time round it will surely be much more as equals travelling the same path together. For me, letter writing still feels more intimate than e-mail, and I'm very glad you feel the same.

Soon Advent will be upon us, season of wonder and waiting for the seed that is God, hidden in the folds of ordinary everyday living. It is the mildest November I can remember, with the birds in a state of confusion, believing it is nest-building time. And yesterday a poppy bloomed in our garden – for myself, always a sign of the Holy Spirit.

All my love and prayers, and gratitude for all He is doing in your life,

Ailsa

ORDINARY TIME

I turn my face to you

from within this seam of ordinary living,

where your people live

day in and day out

hidden with Christ

in the folds of your love,

saints at work

encircling the world,

drawing all men

to the foot of your Cross.

Dearest Kate,

Many thanks for your beautiful card and poem. I was glad to hear you are managing to keep your head above water during the time leading up to Christmas. It is pure grace, together with your cutting down on many of your activities, that you feel blessedly aware of the stillness of Advent amidst the hustle and bustle going on around you. And yes, it is good to be involved with your children at such a time, even when the school concert does become a bit of a marathon!

The local meditation and contemplative prayer group is a great discovery and sounds as if it will be a great help. I am glad your return to the Jesus Prayer* feels like taking up with an old friend. I am sure that is just what it is, for once the prayer has taken root in our heart, it never really leaves us, an echo always remains. This type of prayer, repeating a mantra or a prayer-word, doesn't suit everyone but as you have found, it fits especially well into a busy life where

---

* Repetition of "Lord Jesus Christ [Son of the living God] have mercy upon me [a sinner]."

minds have a problem letting go and becoming still. It quiets us and holds our attention focused, and so keeps us rooted in the present moment. I have heard said of it, "How can you listen to God if you are talking all the time?" which does the Jesus Prayer a great injustice. Rather, it is something we allow to flow through us, eventually becoming hardly more than our breathing. I see the Jesus Prayer as a little like the steel pins inserted in my spine. After the initial operation and allowing time for flesh and sinews to settle and grow around them, they are completely absorbed by my body and hardly noticeable in themselves – yet it is they that keep me standing!

Yes, Kate, if you feel drawn to a shorter form, then go with it. Some of the early contemplatives of the Egyptian desert used just a single word, Jesus, as is suggested also in that great classic, *The Cloud of Unknowing*.

So my prayer for you this Christmas is that circumstances will allow you a window through which you can experience anew the wonder of God as a child in a stable. There is a statue of Mary I saw in Burford Priory – until recently the home of an Anglican Benedicine community – that touches the spot for me, more than many other images we are presented with these days. It captures her on the point of handing her baby into our arms, and with her invitation we find ourselves taken into the heart of mystery. For a moment we see the vulnerability of our God who comes to meet us without any trappings of power. You have begun to say the prayer of abandonment, Kate. But here (and indeed at every Eucharist) we see God giving Himself into our hands...Theologians may write at great length about this, but I am reduced to silence at the immensity of such trust!

Dearest Kate, I wish, for yourself and Pete, Oliver and Harry, a very happy Christmas, and we shall meet in spirit around the altar on Christmas morning.

With continuing love and prayer.

Ailsa

Dearest Kate,

And Happy New Year to you too! It was lovely to find your card waiting for us on our return from New Year at Tymawr, and good to hear that this has been the most enjoyable and least stressful Christmas for you in a long time. New Year's Eve sounded beautiful, with your friends and their families singing Auld Lang Syne in the street beneath the stars. New beginnings do need to be celebrated.

What touched me most was your silent request to God that night, whilst hidden in the company of others: "Make me a clean heart, O God, and renew a right spirit within me." So right for the beginning of a new year – and He will have heard you, Kate, and has a habit of taking us at our word! God will make your heart pure and make you transparent, so that His light can shine through your personality. It will not happen by magic in the blink of an eye, or even without some pain, but gently and gradually through the things that happen to you in the ordinary sameness of work and family life.

One of the monks on Caldey Island tells a wonderful story of when he was a novice. One evening after dark his novice-master beckoned to him to get his cloak, and they walked together up the long road to the lighthouse. When they reached it, the young monk was invited to share his thoughts about the lighthouse but could think of nothing worth saying. His companion said, "That lighthouse saves the lives of hundreds of people it does not even know exist, and the only thing it needs to do is to keep its glass clean." The Jesus Prayer also helps to keep the glass of our souls clean and it was good to hear that it had helped you through the Christmas festivities, even bubbling up of its own accord from time to time.

So, dear Kate, very much a time of thanksgiving and anticipation as you step out into the New Year with your Beloved, resolved to go wherever He may lead. For me, Tymawr was very beautiful in the early light of New Year's morning. It is always a privilege actually to be there, even though they are a constant in my life through the myriad succeeding moments of each day.

With my love, and great thanksgiving at being able to share this part of your journey,

Ailsa

Dear Kate,

Many thanks for your letter. I'm so glad you felt you could write it. You speak of being uneasy about your growing desire to spend more time alone, and not daring to put the label 'solitude' upon it because that feels disloyal and inappropriate for a married person. Yet, my dear, if we say solitude is inappropriate for married people we would have to say that a full relationship with God is inappropriate too! God is a Trinity, but solitude is His environment and silence His language; so any deepening relationship with Him would be very difficult without both of these components.

The trouble is that we have such fixed ideas on this subject, usually associating the search for God with the life of an outsider, a dreamer or an oddity, inhabiting the fringes of society. Such a life may indeed have its own authenticity, but solitude is a necessary part of the human condition of us all, at some level indispensable to any kind of creative living. We can discover it or run from it, in the midst of the competing distractions of life. A quotation from Hesychius in the great book of sayings called *Philokalia*, runs: "You dream of a hermitage, but you already have one here and now. Sit still and cry out, 'Lord, have mercy.'"

Do you remember the little book *Poustinia** that set you on fire when you were a student? If you no longer have it, let me know and I'll send you my copy. It would be well worth reading again now. You probably remember that 'poustinia' is a Russian word for desert or solitude, and the 'poustinik' is someone who goes to be alone, perhaps in a hermitage, in the solitude of woods or fields, and does this not for any personal gain but for the sake of others. Catherine Doherty, born in Russia but living in the west from the age of twenty, was inspired to bring this idea to us in the form of places for quiet retreat – some of them even in the middle of cities. But from there she went even further, to communicate the equally ancient idea of the poustinia of the heart: taking your solitude about with you, even in the market-place, as a pregnant woman carries her child.

Can you relate this to our way of life today, Kate? It is solitude interiorised, albeit needing periods of actual retreat at intervals. You could say it is

---

* Catherine de Hueck Doherty, *Poustinia*, Ave Maria Press 1975; Fount Paperbacks 1977

a space being made by God inside you,where you can live with Him constantly, turning your face to listen to Him, endeavouring to keep it free and empty, available for Him when He comes.

It sounds great, doesn't it? If only it was always as simple as that! So often we feel all the busyness of our lives interferes and works against us in this and it seems to be taking a lifetime to learn – until at last we realise it is not we who are, or can ever be, in control: it is God. Then we begin to find that we are actually given more spaces for solitude than we thought. The physical space and time is there, if we recognise it and are ready and willing to take advantage of it. For instance, a day at home with a minor ailment, when the children are at school and your husband at work, can be turned into a positive gain provided we don't feel too unwell. So can making a train journey and finding we've missed a connection, as long as we don't allow ourselves to get too anxious about the fact. Opportunities will pop up almost daily to sur-prise us and these, together with quiet time consciously built into the day, will help you go deeper into yourself and into God without needing to leave your immediate surroundings.

Eve Baker, married though a member of the Fellowship of Solitaries, says: "The solitary life as it is lived today outside a monastic setting is a profoundly ordinary life. It does not differ in outward appearance from the sort of life lived by everyone else. Like consecrated bread, it is the hidden and invisible element which makes it different."* Creativity in any form is dependent on the artist's acceptance of the limitations of his medium. And so it is for you over the acceptance of family life and work. Like every other human being, you carry within you the possibility of seeing your situation, whatever it is, transformed into something wonderful – the only difference being that not everyone is aware of that possibility. And that awareness is such a precious gift, to be gently held and nurtured. Thomas Merton used to say, "We exist solely for this – to be the human place God has chosen for His presence, His manifestation in the world."

Perhaps that's enough for now. Of course there will be more – there always is with God – but maybe it is best not to try to anticipate Him. I am just off for a walk around the nature reserve at the back of our cottage: opportunity for solitude in a very natural and healthy form?!

With my love and prayer always,

Ailsa

---

* *Paths in Solitude*, St Pauls (UK) 1995

Sweet solitude –
sister of mine,
in whose company I am free
to breathe and to be myself,
before whom I can stand
naked
defenceless
and vulnerable
without fear of hurt or of hurting;

friendship with you
is my gateway to intimacy,
and together
we prepare a place for His homing,
making ready a welcome
to greet Him
when He comes:

a place
where a king may find comfort
disguised as a beggar
and where always
balm of pure nard stands ready
on the table.

There is a garden

secluded and enclosed

where my Lord has chosen we shall meet:

a place of shade, out of the heat of the day,

where he allows me to welcome him,

to sit at his feet,

drink the wine of his presence

and wash his feet with my tears.

Dear Kate,

It was good to hear you managed a long half-term weekend in London *en famille* and that you all enjoyed the London Eye so much. I always love visiting London. I think of it as the other end of a piece of string stretching from Pembrokeshire! So good for the boys too, at their age; and as you say, it's an important part of their education, if only to learn how to use the Underground.

Your poems are beautiful. Please keep them coming; they are a wonderful mode of expression and communication. You describe this new beginning in your spiritual journey as like a kind of coming home to yourself, as if it has been germinating under the surface all these years, and I am sure it has, Kate. You say ideas like the poustinia excite you, but you are grateful for my comments on the struggle because it all seems more difficult to put into practice this time round. Now, it is not only yourself and God you have to consider, but your family and friends and pupils and all the details of everyday life, so that you can't help asking, "Is this prayer journey even possible, for people in my situation?"

Dear Kate, my immediate and heart-felt reply to your question – and I believe you already know the answer – is that if it is not for you, then it is not for anybody! All that is on offer to a contemplative nun is on offer to you too. Having a relationship with God is not an elitist occupation, dependent on having the 'right' circumstances and context to live in. Rather, it depends entirely on His generosity and is open to all of us, in and through the very circumstances in which we find ourselves.

More and more I am coming to appreciate that this journey of love is, in fact, one of enlightenment, of growing into recognition of what in a sense, already exists. Thomas Merton's answer to the question, "How best can we help people attain union with God?" is, "We must tell them they are already with God." "Contemplative prayer", he says, "is nothing more than the coming into consciousness of what is already there." Part of this process is realising that everything we experience *belongs*, every aspect of our life is truly an aspect of our spiritual journey. There is a familiar saying that I know I've quoted to you before – it's picked up by Daniel O'Leary in his book *Travelling Light* which I have only just been reading – "All is harvest." So, Kate, the demands on you to attend to others – especially Pete and the boys – and the consequent struggle you have to find time alone, not to mention the apparent impossibility of remaining consciously in God's presence – all these things are part and parcel of the same search. It isn't as if He hands out to everyone a 'one-size-fits-all' ready-made uniform we have to fit into if we are to grow closer to Him, but that each one of us is offered a garment individually woven to fit our own particular personality and life.

You know this, really, Kate. Deep within yourself you understand that there is no duality between family and spiritual life, rather that this is the arena in which God will nurture your awareness of Him. Your personal circumstances are in fact your greatest resource, and you will meet Him not in spite of them but, mysteriously, through them. Time alone with Him is important, but it's good to remember that it is actually impossible *not* to be in the presence of God, whether we are aware of it or not! All the major religions unite in their insistence that learning this lesson IS the journey we speak of. "Be awake!" they constantly exhort us. As one of the Desert Fathers (Father Lazarus) puts it, "Wakefulness of the spirit is a blessing for the world; and to stay awake means struggle!"

On that note, very dear Kate, I am off to the garden for the first time this year, to see what delights God has in store: the first crocuses, perhaps?

Always with great love and prayer,

Ailsa

Dearest Kate,

I do enjoy receiving your letters! They push me to articulate thoughts and feelings sometimes previously unchallenged, and I am grateful for that. It is also a joy and a privilege to be alongside you as you continue to follow the Light wherever it leads.

I have been specially aware of you this past week, and it cannot be a coincidence that I am sitting down to answer your last letter the day after attending a 'Cloister Day' at St David's Cathedral on the Desert Fathers. It was such a beautiful subject and the day was brilliantly led by Patrick Thomas. Best of all, because it was out of season, the whole place was empty of all but the most stalwart of pilgrims, so that the Cathedral herself was hushed and seemed to be at prayer. I was very conscious of you and your puzzle as to how to move on without the scope to practise the life of ordered asceticism that monks and nuns deliberately choose. Now we are really getting down to the nitty-gritty of God's creativity in coming up with a custom-made suit for every individual!

The fact is, Kate, that the stripping away of what is superfluous is always part of the spiritual journey, for those not called to live a life apart, as much as for those who are; but "what is superfluous" can be different from one person to another. The same challenge to grow spiritually comes to us in different forms, depending on our life-circumstances. As we have said before, if we could only see the whole of life as one big 'monastery' or 'school of love' set up for us by God, then we would recognise that the natural flow of the events of our lives provides for us all the discipline and stripping we could need to live out the depth of commitment you long for.

This was brought home to me some time ago, when I was privileged to have access to a programme of reflection and study set up by the Cistercian Order of monks and nuns on the historic documents (the 'Exordium') of their own foundation. At first reading, I could not see much with which I could identify at all. But then for the word 'cell' I substituted 'heart' – and the whole work came to life. Outwardly, the Cistercian Order is characterised by separation from the world, but inwardly their goal is exactly the same as ours, the pursuit of the life of contemplative prayer which will bring us ever closer to God. The goal in fact is love and the 'imitation of Christ' by monks and nuns when they make vows of poverty, chastity and obedience is not adopted as an end in itself but in order to "light the fire of love for the Bridegroom".

Saint Bernard, the twelfth-century Cistercian Abbot, told his monks: "Get rid of the non-essentials and life-giving options will present themselves." You have spontaneously been doing your own 'spring-cleaning' of your life, Kate. Beyond that, you will find that for those of us not called to monastic life there is still plenty of opportunity for practising poverty – being 'poor with the poor Christ' – just as long as we do not try to compensate by turning to distractions. Poverty can in reality mean many things: lack of space or silence, tiredness, loneliness, are only a few of the possible privations... So the monastics have no special status by reason of their way of life. Mother Mary Jean at Tymawr Convent surely has it right when she says, "We are all in this together." As far as our destination is concerned, there is only one journey for us all to make. While the actual paths to the destination are innumerable, no one path does a better job than any other. Each fulfils its role, providing a way for the traveller to reach the place of heart's desire.

The wonderful wisdom of the fathers and mothers of the desert I was hearing about yesterday is given us, and equally that of their modern-day counterparts, to help us become grounded in faith and in our relationship with God: until we finally learn we have no need of any special life-situation to support it – it has become 'interiorised' within us. Especially important is their teaching about staying put, thus giving oneself the chance to go deeper; and about living within the given parameters of our lives, yet being true to oneself and to Christ. They emphasise that the ingredients of our own personal world are the way, the only way, for us to meet God, and for Him to meet us. While they encourage us to incorporate silence, stillness and solitude into our daily life as much as we can, they also suggest that in the midst of noise and busyness God is still there and that if we stop fretting about our need for quiet, we may even be able to glimpse Him, so to speak, in the dishwasher or the shopping trolley!

One day we must visit St David's together, and as well as wandering the cloisters I will treat you to lunch in the newly-created restaurant there. Jesus may have fasted in the desert, but He also enjoyed the wine at the wedding-party in Cana of Galilee!

My love and prayer as always,

Ailsa

My dear Kate,

I was wondering why I had not heard from you for so long and was getting a little anxious. I'm all the more grateful that you have felt able to write so fully to tell me what has been happening and the dark place you are now in. I am so sorry that – though you had hinted at it – I didn't realise how deeply the difficult relationship with your headmaster had been eating away at you. And of course I understand that in the aftermath of that disastrous day before Easter you've felt quite unable to pick up your pen and write about it, until now.

Believe me, it isn't at all uncommon to come to a stage in our walk with God when suddenly the "shadow side" of life rises up and confronts us with extra force. You have done so well to hold down your teaching job up to this point and not buckle under the strain, especially when you have been at such close quarters with the source of your anguish all this time.

As I understand it, this headmaster seemed to have it in for you, as they say, from the moment he arrived at the school five years ago, and has subjected you to continual criticism and put-down, with never a word of encouragement or praise. Despite your excellent reputation as a teacher, abundantly demonstrated throughout your career, this man somehow has the ability not just to undermine your confidence but totally to disempower you, by his refusal to acknowledge the worth of your best efforts.

And then at the end of term you were asked, as usual, to help the children put on a classroom presentation of the Easter story at Assembly, with all the staff and parents there; and in the middle of all their congratulations and compliments to you afterwards, the Head broke in and said coldly, "I see you forgot to let the caretaker know about the extra parking area we needed to open up for this morning" – and that was just the final straw. You felt totally demolished, contrived to cover it until you got home, but have barely managed to cope with any aspect of life since.

It's always very frightening when your feelings overwhelm you in this way and you are so completely squashed, trodden underfoot – especially when you recognise that your reaction is out of all proportion to the incident itself. It leaves you unable to understand what is happening to you, and I am not at all surprised that you have felt shaken and tearful ever since, and are now obliged to ask your doctor for sick leave rather than go back straight away to school after the Easter break. The kind of dripfeed of criticism you have been subjected to can be enough to break down the strongest personality, when it is prolonged and comes from someone holding the reins of power. And every one of us has some particular vulnerable, tender area which is liable to further damage from treatment such as you have received. I wish I could be alongside to put my arms round you and say something that would comfort. As it is, I will have to ask the Lord to give me words that might be some help from a distance.

Dear Kate, I do believe that you will one day see this black period as a very important part of your spiritual journey. Hard as it may be to imagine now, there will come a time when you can look back on what has happened and see that even here, in this awfulness, God was – is – present. In fact it is often only when we feel things couldn't be worse that our woundedness is really opened up for God to heal. So what He asks of you now is to do your best to hang in there, trusting Him in the darkness. Do you recall the story of the Israelites wandering in the desert? Frequently tempted to lose hope, they realised later on that "God carried them all the way, as a father carries a child". Throughout their years of weary trudging, all their needs had been supplied, their sandals never wore out – He enabled them to keep on going.

I will stop here, Kate, for the time being, because this is a long letter and your energies must be very low. Just know that I am here for you. Feel free to write, but don't feel you have to.

With all my love,

Ailsa

Dear Kate,

You have such courage! I'm glad what I wrote last time carried some little glimmers of light to you and gave you a sense of a guide-rope to hang on to in the darkness. When we are given grace to accept our brokenness rather than try any longer to fight it – which seems to be what has happened to you in the last few days – that is when things can begin to shift and a small space is cleared for some whispers of God's peace to filter in to you. He is here, in this situation as in every other we could ever encounter in our lives: we've talked of that so often before. For now, the only thing to do is to say, "Lord, I believe" or at least, "Lord, I want to believe"; and to wait, with as much trust as we can, in the face of mystery. "This is how I am. This is how it is. I don't understand but I accept it. In your own good time, Lord, you will show me as much as I need to understand of why it has happened, why it is so."

At some point most of us come to a Gethsemane of our own, as Jesus did. Saying that, I don't at all mean to imply that in this particular situation your duty is to shoulder the role of 'victim' and resign yourself to taking what has happened lying down. If it isn't possible for you to move to another school, a way has to be found to deal with this unmanageable relationship where you are now. But could it be that God, in this very crisis, is drawing you on to another, still richer stage of your journey with Him? Much as Jesus' struggle in Gethsemane would prove to be the way to a harvest at the time utterly beyond anyone's imagining? I believe you mentioned realising even as it happened that the strength of your reaction to that 'final straw' moment was far greater than the actual situation warranted. It might give a clue to the way forward if you could search your memory a bit: can you recall ever feeling anything like this before, on some smaller scale? Also, I wonder if it has ever occurred to you that your Head might see you, consciously or not, as in some way a threat to him, perhaps by the very fact of your being so good at your job?

Still, questions of that kind mustn't be your chief focus right now. Thinking along those lines needs to be from within your trust in God's sheltering embrace, even if you cannot feel that for what it is just now. The book I am currently reading by Martin Laird, *Into the Silent Land*, says that the sense of God's absence is an illusion: we are and always have been, united to Him, regardless of whether we perceive the fact or not. Our moods and feelings, he says, are "as weather on the holy mountain. And we are not the weather; we are the mountain." God is our still centre, and your journey there is one on which God will accompany you, willing and loving you into His infinite peace.

Dear Kate, I shall be holding you and all the family daily in that silence and stillness, as best as I can. Write or phone whenever you want to.

With constant love and prayer,

Ailsa

How different it all is when Summer goes
and the first chill of Autumn
cools the ardour of those heady love-long days;
passion past spending,
your features fade into the mellowing mist
and silence settles
on the flaming fire of our love.

And yet ...
      glowing embers
      reflect
      the richness of the cooling earth
and there is promise
      in the bulging branch –
      with hint of other passion yet to come.
The burnish'd beauty of your going
holds a promise and a pain that's all its own.

WINTER

With the world tilting into Winter
and nature slipping silent into nakedness,
you took me away
(as young men do before war)
to a secret place
to be alone with you.
In time that stood still –
when now is forever –
you showered me with kisses
and spoke of love that will not change its mind.

And now it is Winter
and iced winds blow
round the places of our loving
as cold chills the spaces left empty
by your going.

I cry for you
and wait...
Wait, like the women who wait,
living and longing,
awaiting only your return
warmed by your love even in your absence,
hugging our secret
close to my heart.

Dearest Kate,

It was good to have your letter and to hear that Pete and the boys are being so supportive. And what beautiful poems you sent! They are more moving than ever. Somehow, even while you feel the absence of God so keenly, deep inside you recognise that to be aware of His absence is itself a kind of affirming of His reality, His continuing hidden presence. You express that so well and it tempers the bleakness of the situation. I agree entirely that the greatest fear of modern man is that all is ultimately meaningless.

You ask me whether what is happening to you is the kind of thing St John of the Cross writes about, or whether that is something on a different level altogether, experienced only by a handful of the greatest souls, all of them people who have lived under the strict ascetic discipline of a monastery or a convent. I can tell you without any doubt that John is speaking of a type of experience which may come to anyone at all who genuinely seeks to find and know God. But John has much to say about 'dark night' and it can never be reduced to one neat definition, if only because, as individuals, we register and interpret our experience in such different terms. What you are going through is undoubtedly a dark night for you, in the sense that you feel cut off from God. What John would say is that the very events which have brought you to this state may also be, with God, one of the greatest blessings of your life. This is because for John, to have to walk in darkness means to have to walk in faith. And it is only through faith, not through concrete evidence, that we can come to 'know' God with our deepest selves and our whole being – rather than just knowing about God and trying to use all sorts of needless or outgrown bits of 'evidence' to bolster our faith in Him. It is like clinging on to the water-wings, not daring to throw them away. We can't prove we don't need them any more, until the moment we take them off and swim!

As you are beginning to see, Kate, the form our experience takes is intimately bound up with the core of who we are and the particular pattern of ordinary daily life we happen to follow. Periods of blockage and 'desolation' or 'aridity' (to use the technical terms) happen to even the most thick-skinned of us, in one fashion or other. What we do with those is what counts, and that can often mean looking at how we are reacting to them, and at why we have encountered them in this particular shape and form. (I've already suggested you might think about how your relationship with your headmaster came to provoke in you a reaction last term that you know was hugely out of proportion to what he said and the situation in which he said it.)

Sadly, because of the very depth and complexity of his thought many people don't give St John of the Cross a chance. They dismiss his writings out of hand as irrelevant to modern life or only for the very, very few. This is such a pity, because John can be a good friend and a trusty guide, most of all when we find ourselves faced with an abyss of meaninglessness. He tells us that life does have meaning even when we can't see it, exhorting us at those times to trust that God can see when we can't. He tells us that negative things in our lives, such as your present experience of being trodden underfoot, are all part of an adventure of love. We actually need them, because the space or emptiness they make in us allow God the room to enter our inner world. Speaking from his own experience of rejection, even physical imprisonment by others, John does not romanticise anything but encourages us to be open to ways of using our suffering creatively. And so he sees the darkness we want to escape as being in fact a great opportunity for us to receive the gift which is God Himself. He meets his Beloved in the night, not after it.

It is so tempting and natural to run from hurt, and we do just that in so many ways, but if we can stay with it and wait, as I believe you are able to do, Kate, then the God who seeks us far more eagerly than we seek Him will fill you with Himself. This is God's enterprise, and the abyss we face is not in the end one of meaninglessness but of Love. Does that sound remote and far-fetched? I believe we often don't truly think of God as real, and definitely not that He is really concerned about the details of our lives! But John of the Cross is obsessed with this great love God has for us. Our task, he says is not to set out to achieve anything, but to try and let go, be emptied out in order to receive God Himself into that space.

Forgive me if all this is just too much. I love you dearly and want the stillness of these weeks at home to strengthen you. Perhaps it will help to repeat from time to time:

> *Circle me, O God,*
> *keep stillness within,*
> *keep turmoil out.*

>> *Circle me, O God,*
>> *keep trust within,*
>> *keep fear without.*

>>> *Circle me, O God,*
>>> *keep love within,*
>>> *all that is not love – out.*

The heron that flies across our garden each morning returned this evening – with a friend! Spring is obviously well under way.

With my love always, and daily prayer,

Ailsa

THE STORM

Relentless,

rain falls heavy on the flowers of the mind;

as the thunder roars louder round the corners
of the spirit.

Lightning – flashes of fear

illumine the emptiness and devastation
accomplished.

Uprooted and helpless,

the delicate flowers are washed away

in the frenzy of nature's emotion.

With them goes life

and meaning

and identity.

All is desolate,

all is void,

all is nothing.

Then, from beyond the storm,

the outstretched arms

and the still, small voice:

"I will be all in your nothingness."

My dear Kate,

Your powerful 'Storm' poem arrived today, and I couldn't help hoping that its ending reflects something of the course of our phone conversation last night. It was good to talk to you then, and I hope you ended up rather less frightened and were able to sleep.

I do understand how terrifying it is to feel that what is going on inside you is beyond your control – a much more fearful situation than being caught up in some physical event, a tornado, say, or a train crash, that tears up your outer environment. But I hope I was able to reassure you that this experience is not a sign of madness, still less of some weakness of character that is crippling you; it is just a part of being human. I wish with all my heart and soul I could take it from you; yet I know it is somehow within God's loving plan for you, an invitation, a place of opportunity.

Dear Kate, however painful it is right now, you have arrived at the very heart of everything we have talked about in the realm of spiritual life and relationship with God. Control is a small word but we treat the actual thing as a huge, indispensable tool that we must hang on to at all costs. The loss of it fills us with utter dread. Do you know which words are most often used in the gospels for that situation? It is: "Do not be afraid", spoken by angels, and even more frequently by Jesus Himself. These are the words He is speaking to you today, Kate: He is asking you to trust Him enough to hand over your life, and with it your helplessness, to Him, to His control. Scary stuff! And yet, the 'night' described by John of the Cross, when it seems to overtake us, requires a 'yes' from us before it can become, in his word, 'blessed'. If and when we are ready to give that 'yes', there will still be a lifetime's work for us, learning to allow God to have full rein. Only little by little can we get used to letting the Holy Spirit lead us, in all the details of our doings from day to day. It is our willingness that is everything.

The Cistercian fathers of old, like so many other spiritual guides, remind us constantly that we are never really 'in control' of our lives, because we depend entirely on God. His initiative always comes first. Ours is only the responsibility and the free choice to respond to Him. That makes it sound easy, and so it would be, if only we didn't find it so hard to believe that this invisible God truly wants the best for us, even more than we want it for ourselves!

I don't want you to misunderstand me, Kate. This kind of surrender to God doesn't lead to a comfortable life in which you can sit back and not do anything because God has got it all sorted. Rather, a new dimension is opened up for us. We can hear much better than before, in the events and circumstances of our life, the 'still, small voice' that speaks to us of what God wants. And gradually listening for His gentle approaches, "Come this way", spoken throughout the day, can become for us a way of life. He only asks us to trust that He is in charge of the natural flow of our lives, the ups and downs – even when every shred of goodness or meaning may be hidden from us. One of Anthony de Mello's sayings that I love runs: "Said the river to the seeker, 'Do I really have to fret about enlightenment? No matter which way I turn, I am homeward bound!'"

My dear Kate, I believe God is giving you an opportunity now to say 'Yes' to Him at a deeper level than before: to believe that He holds your whole situation in His hands and will by His mysterious power somehow turn it into blessing.

With my love and continuing prayer,

Ailsa

PS Do you remember the poem of yours we included at the end of *Letters to Kate*? It was one you wrote at the end of your time in college, when you were just about to go off to do voluntary service, teaching in Africa – a great launch into the unknown. I'm sending you a copy, so you don't even have to hunt for it, as it is so very apt and poignant for where you are now. Your outward circumstances are so different, but the trust and the gift of self that are being asked of you are one and the same, only at a much deeper level of your being. The invitation always entails risk – sometimes, seemingly, risking our all – in a step of faith which costs "not less than everything". But when we take that step, the darkness can by grace be turned to light.

UNKNOWN COUNTRY

The way stretches ahead
from within this place
and moment of time,
wayless,
unformed,
with no light in its darkness.

And what else is there to do
when led through unknown country
at night
by a guide who goes his own way,
keeping his thoughts to himself?
What else, but to put yourself in his hands?

Past all points of no return,
with no bird in the hand
should the two in the bush get away,
I stake my life on your promise
and, taking your hand,
plunge headlong into the all-embracing darkness.

Dearest Kate,

Thank you for your wonderful letter. I'm so glad the poem fitted the place you were at, but still more that you are feeling better. The greatest news, though, is your finding yourself enabled to say 'yes' – however apprehensively you say it was given.

And then there is the account of your "epiphany moment", which "doesn't change anything, yet changes everything." As you say, such insights sometimes seem to burst on us out of nowhere, suddenly and with great clarity, and this one seems to be not only a revelation to you but the key to so much. You have realised that the reason your headmaster's judgmental attitude and actual criticisms have held so much power over you is because this is just how you felt about your relationship with your father when you were growing up. Here it was, happening all over again. You were being relentlessly dis-empowered, caught in a familiar spiral of hurt, but not making the mental connection with your early life experience that is now so obvious.

It can be quite a jolt to the system when these insights surface for us. But this is certainly one of the ways the light of the Holy Spirit answers our prayers, whether those were explicit or simply our desperate, inarticulate last-gasp cries. God allows us to experience again the kind of hurt that clouded our earlier years, but only up to the point when we are able to recognise it and hold it up for healing to His light. This is an immensely important discovery for you and I can understand your saying you can almost feel yourself growing! There lives on within everyone a very young self, often deeply hurt, though often quite unintentionally, in the very process of growing to adulthood. Maturity involves recognising and befriending this child and offering understanding and healing, through love, almost as if this were someone outside our own skin, yet still 'us'. How often have we heard it said – we cannot truly love anyone else until and unless we learn to love ourselves?

It will take time to practise listening to your 'inner child', and understanding her, Kate, but during that time she will be teaching you, too. You will learn from her the qualities of childhood that Jesus said were vital for us to enter His kingdom: trust, simplicity, an uncomplicated humility, with a sense of wonder and no need to feel important. At the same time we must remember that Jesus tells us to become like a little child – not revert to being one! It is growth we are concerned with, and a journey towards a wholeness which is holiness: not a return to an out-of-place childishness, but the integration of this hurt little child into our adult personhood.

Very dear Kate, you have had the courage to stay with the pain of your situation, and now God has broken through the darkness with this wonderful shaft of His healing light and love. With it comes the gift of recognising this as a big step forward on the path you have wished to take – the path to Him. And it is my great privilege to be alongside you as it happens.

With constant love and prayer,

Ailsa

Dearest Kate,

It was really heartwarming to have your account of your lovely June day out in the countryside with Pete. He has clearly been a great help and support to you all the way through, and it's not surprising that you feel more and more appreciative as the days go by. I smiled when you said, "I think he's one of those we're always talking about – the unacknowledged saints who would laugh in your face if you told them that's what they are!"

Yes, of course it is a shock to you to realise you are not as 'together' a person as you thought you were. But you have taken this insight on board and begun to accept the woundedness within, and that is so important. Without it, our spiritual journeying is hugely hampered or can even come to a halt. Somehow we have to face up to the reality of the person we are, rather than the one we would like to be, knowing that God loves the person we are, while the person we aren't is a figment. This is not to do with low self-esteem, but with realising that we are all flawed and wounded in one way or another. The present Dalai Lama says, "It is our suffering that is the

64

most basic element we share with others, the factor that unites us with all living creatures." The pain of our own particular form of woundedness is the personal 'cross' we are asked to accept. And often that gives no sign at all that any good can possibly come of it! How can feeling beaten down and battered be anything to do with entering into fuller life? In de Caussade's parable the piece of stone being sculpted has no idea what it is destined to become, it is only aware of its present experience – the pain being inflicted by the chisel.

So with you now, Kate. It will need time fully to arrive on the other side of this unexpected crumpling of your defences; but whatever it takes, however much it hurts, all this is part of God's liberating and strengthening action. The Holy Spirit may be doing His best work at the moments when we feel worst. We can never see this until we look back afterwards. But if we could see it at the time, we would almost certainly relax our efforts to keep our eyes on God and learn what He is teaching us: the naked faith that has to be there if He is fully to heal us, to make us whole, which is one description of what redemption means.

Like the stillness at the centre of the whirlwind, at the central core of your pain is a great silence. It is this place that you have glimpsed and are heading for. There you will find yourself united with all others in their pain, but also – and this blows the mind! – with Christ in His Passion. In this process of being redeemed we become partakers with Christ in His work: our own small wounds become part of a great mystery. Sheila Cassidy is often quoted in this context: "I believe no pain is lost. The blood shed in Salvador will irrigate the heart of some financier a million miles away."

If that doesn't sound very convincing to you, Kate, never mind! It's really my own deepest convictions finding expression. If you would like me to, I could try to unpack it a bit further, but it isn't at all needful. We don't need to know the horticultural detail to appreciate the beauty of a rose. The nub of it all is that our wounds are good teachers. It truly will be possible, one day, to be genuinely grateful for the very hurt and damage you have suffered – from your father and headmaster both; because this will have been for you a doorway opening up on new, unlooked-for riches. The poet Jay Parini says it beautifully in *The Uses of Sorrow*: "Someone once gave me a box full of darkness. It took me years to understand that this, too, was a gift."

This isn't the first time I feel the need to apologise in case I have overloaded you, Kate! But you know that every word that comes from your aging godmother carries with it my love to you. I am so glad you have been able to continue with your prayer-times and so keep open the path to your inner centre where the Lord reigns in His peace.

All my love and prayer,

Ailsa

My dear Kate,

Many thanks for your letter. It's great that you feel well enough to plan to return to school for the final week of this term, to test your "sea-legs" well in advance of the new school year. And thank you for assuring me that my letter helped rather than hindered you in the ongoing task of making sense of these last weeks – actually getting on for three months, isn't it, by now? You are plainly on much firmer inner ground now than you were, though you are bound still to feel wobbly and vulnerable after so much time out, and to see the prospect of going into school as like braving the lion's den. Deeper understanding takes much of the bite out of potentially hurtful situations, but the power of the past is hard to deal with. "Is it going to happen all over again?" Best not to try and grit your teeth and stand in your own newfound strength, but plug into your greatest resource, as St Paul did. "Three times I asked the Lord to take this thing from me, but He said to me, 'My strength is sufficient for you, for my power is made perfect in weakness.'"

To follow Jesus means that we must learn to be compassionate as He was. But true compassion is not possible unless we know what vulnerability feels like. In this sense it is part of our calling to 'be vulnerable', not to be closed off from others and content behind our own ramparts. Like true humility, though, this is not a virtue easily won, – and not, as we've said, to do with either child-ish naiveté or with false modesty and a pride in making ourselves into martyrs. The way of Jesus is the way of love, honesty and truth, and it was simply the undeflected walking of this way which brought Him to surrender Himself willingly into the hands of others while He was on earth. The greatest wonder is that He continues even now to do the very same thing: at every Eucharist He makes Himself small, puts Himself totally at my mercy. What incredible trust! And he asks me to be willing to be equally trusting in regard to my friend and my foe, if I am to walk His way.

As He was with us, so are we meant to be ready to 'abandon' ourselves (in de Caussade's word) to others; at the deepest level to be open to the people and the circumstances that we encounter at every moment of every day. This is hard. It hurts! We so often hit out in reflex counter-attack or draw back in self-protection and close ourselves off. Christ asks us not to do this but to keep on trying to stay aware and open to others, not only to their goodness and generosity, but to their quirkiness, their brokenness – just however and whoever they are.

I can almost see you flinching, Kate! Your pain is still too raw, and in any case this is a lifetime's programme, not the work of a week or two. I believe what I am really wanting to say to you is that these months have brought you into a new understanding of what it could mean to speak of "Christ within you". It is out of this very experience that you will gradually find yourself more and more able to bear the pain involved in being open, potentially vulnerable, to others. It will gradually become much less painful for you because you are becoming stronger, more healed, more whole – and therefore better able to help others in their own kinds of pain.

Dear Kate, He loves you and I love you, and will be keeping you specially close to my heart in the days you are back at school. Meanwhile, one final favourite thought (I don't know where it comes from) which has always rejoiced my heart and spurred me on – especially when I found it hard to stay open-hearted to people who snubbed or seemed to want to belittle me:

> *He drew a circle and shut me out –*
> *rebel, heretic, thing to flout.*
> *But Love and I had the wit to win:*
> *we drew a circle and drew him in!*

With all my love and prayers,

Ailsa

Dearest Kate,

I was so glad to hear from you – of course my thoughts have never been far from you during this last week, back in the school environment even if not fully back in the usual timetable of teaching. It could only be a very testing time for you, and it's heartening to hear that the staff have borne your long absence with such warm sympathy and welcomed you back with open arms. I can imagine something of the inner quivering you would feel when you faced your Head, though, wondering if everything would straight away revert to the old pattern.

So I'm more than pleased with what you say about these days. Granted his first greeting was a bit frosty, it was at least polite (he must, after all, have found it hard to manage this last term without your skill and experience at his disposal for classes). Then you talked a bit with him about timetabling for next year, and he began to pour cold water on your suggestions and implied that you "weren't standing up to the pressures of teaching very well any more" and therefore your ideas weren't worth consideration – but where in the past you would have crumpled and found yourself silenced, completely thrown, this time you were able calmly (and with at least the semblance of confidence!) to hold your ground and make your point. Well, all I can say is "Brilliant!" This is great news and you must feel it's a good omen for the future.

Of course there will be many moments, as there were even this week, of "wobble" and slipping back into the victim-role. But you have gained a vital understanding now. You know that the habitual attitudes which have become like second nature to us, a skin we could never shed, can truly be changed, once we recognise them. Of ourselves we are helpless to kill them off by force: they are like persistent weeds, constantly regrowing. But if we are prepared gently and consistently to keep on countering them every time we realise they are poking their heads up again, they will gradually die back – at least lose their strength and their stranglehold, though we always have to watch out for regrowth. And you have made here a crucial connection. The process of change, of greater self-knowledge, begins in the silence of prayer, in steadily returning to that place you are getting to know again, after so long: the place of silence far deeper inside yourself than surface anxieties, deeper than the attitudes so much part of you since childhood. This is where you can encounter God, commune, in words or not, with Christ. Here is where true inner strength can begin to grow.

Trust this deep place, Kate. If sometimes nothing seems to happen or you feel reluctant to go there at all – perhaps when your outer life is extra problematic, tense, or just 'grey' – don't be tempted to think this newfound strength in Christ is an illusion. Have the courage to say to yourself, "Yes, what happened this Spring was real and I am going to go on living by that conviction. I know there may still come times when I feel trodden down, at a loss, not able to make sense of my moods and reactions. But I know that then to wait in faith, to stay with the silence and not-knowing, will bring me – in God's good time – to new insights, deeper wisdom, finding a way through. And I will know that these are His direct answer to my need and to my wish to give my whole life into His loving hands, to use for good in whatever way He wills."

By this attitude we gradually reconcile the conflict between our child and our (more!) adult selves, diminish the constant rocking between leaning on others more than we should, and insisting that we get our own way, preserve our own independence and control of things and people. In this life we never become all that with God's help we could be. But the rewards of trying to make that journey wholeheartedly outweigh by far any trials and struggles that come to us in the course of it!

And soon I shall have that rare treat, your company here in our cottage for a whole week! I am sorry that the niggling back trouble you've been having means that you can't accompany Pete and the boys on their coastal walk – the Pembrokeshire Path is wonderful at any time of year, but especially in any halfway decent summer! But their loss is my and David's gain. He joins me, by the way, in saying how delighted he is you are coming. He's always had a soft spot for you, you know. He wasn't at all put out when it dawned on us that the week before you come we were having our youngest grand-daughter Charlotte and a friend of hers to stay. That is a real tribute to you, as he tends to like a 'breather' between visitors coming, if possible.

Looking forward so much to seeing you, I send great love, as always,

Ailsa

My dear Kate,

What a happy week we had! I feel like a cat that has had almost too much cream, yet I'm energised by the sheer delight our spirits found in each other's company. What a treasure-trove of discoveries shared and new trails opening up for mind and heart.

And Pete and Oliver and Harry will have all those photos of their equally invigorating trail along our beloved Pembrokeshire Coastal Path. Pete is a great father as well as husband, isn't he? And David was so interested to see where they had been, and loved telling them all his tales – the legends and stories about the local characters and the landmarks.

Speaking of fathers – and even of another Harry, as it happens – I was very interested by your mentioning one day the unexpected questions you found you were asking yourself about God when the children were very small. Later, this reminded me of an occasion long, long ago when I had the nerve to write to the author Harry Williams about something of the sort and had the most wonderful letter back from him. I made a mental note to look it out, and will share it with you when I find it; I know it's safe somewhere in the house.

I hope you will find your back is holding up once you are 'into the groove' at home again with the domestic chores and so on. Hopefully the last three weeks of the holiday, with the help of your programme at the gym, should build up your strength so that you have all the backbone you need – physical as well as spiritual! – to return to the full régime at school next term.

Kate, I think I appreciate our friendship across a generation more and more, as the days go by. Thank you and bless you. I chose to write straight after your stay so that I could send this little poem as a memento of your visit and our morning strolls. If it seems slightly tinged with hurt not long past, it's definitely about hope, trust and healing happening now!

Your ever-loving godmother,

Ailsa

Midsummer morning after a night of
        torrential rain

and the Pembrokeshire lanes lie freshly
        laundered,

held in a stillness

like the aftermath of pain.

The foxgloves are brighter today,

newly painted in the morning mist;

and joy shouts from the banks of the way –

still wet with tears,

but sheltered by the overhanging branches
        of your care.

Dear Kate,

This comes hot on the heels of my last missive, because I've finally turned up the treasured letter from Harry Williams. I'll have to explain the background a bit.

You'll remember that one afternoon when you were here you told me about the inner questioning that went on in you for a while when the boys were young. Your faith in God had pretty much faded into the background under all the pressures at that time, with Pete very stretched in his job and you back to fulltime teaching once Harry and Oliver were old enough to be at school. It wouldn't be surprising if you began to wonder whether God was real, or just a nice idea that humankind had thought up, way back, as wish-fulfilment – for reassurance in a world that can be very harsh, or to meet the need for Something or Someone to pray to, a need which seems to be inbuilt in us. It would be logical to invent a God who was a larger-than-life ideal father. Faced with that image, a young person like you, who didn't feel much trust in her actual father, would be all too easily persuaded that God existed – even if He didn't. She would 'need' to believe it.

But there is another side to it. Supposing the Father-God exists, but isn't in fact the wished-for good, kind father-figure at all. Perhaps the real God is as dominating and demanding as you felt your own father to be, constantly squashing and under-valuing you! So you had two questions. The first was, "Is God real?" The second was, "If He is real, what is He really like – is the popular image true? If it isn't, if He's actually stern and harsh, it seems that believing in Him can't be much help to me! Am I prepared to trust what they say about Him being good?"

Many people ask themselves questions of that kind. I did that very same thing when I was young, but when I came across Harry Williams' book *The True Wilderness*, I was bowled over by it and as I told you, plucked up courage to write to him. He wrote back this wonderful reply which I share with you: "God is neither father nor mother, but He gives us images in which to think of Himself. In this case, God Himself is the picture-slasher, and in His own good time He will give you another image in which to think of Him. So don't worry that your dolls have been put in the dustbin. In His own good time God will give you a pony!" Isn't that wonderful! He was such a humble man, and knew all about the struggle for faith. But he certainly put my worries about images of God into proper perspective. If we have the courage to put our faith in Him, we may find our doubts soon fade away for ever. Anyway, I'd love to hear your comments. You may have a different take on Harry Williams' words from mine.

By the way, I haven't yet received the poems you promised me. Please don't forget to send them! – especially the two you mentioned on our way to picnic at St Non's, but didn't actually show me – perhaps you felt they ran too deep for the flow of such a lovely, lighthearted day out?

My love and prayers to you – hoping to hear from you soon.

Ailsa

MOMENT IN TIME

A moment in time
that cannot be captured
or held in the hand,
only lived,
then let go
at the turn of the tide.

On this sea-shore of stillness
the only souind is
love-lapping,
the might of the ocean
round these stones
through my soul.

A cliff-cloistered corner,
remotest reach
of creation -
and the gentleness of God
Christ-caressing
the soul.

HERE

Here where the cliffs stoop to greet the ocean

and gulls swoop screeching across a shimmering
        silver sea,

time stands still

held

hovering

in an eternity that is now.

And just for a moment

you show me,

as the mist rises

and distance dilates,

something of the mystery

that streams between heaven and earth.

Your cross stands out against a cloudless sky,
stark symbol of suffering
transformed in love
and surrounded now by joy,
blazing, burnished gold of gorse
sprung from the very heart of hopelessness.

And it's here that you draw me,
longing, waiting, patient for my 'yes',
my pain to meet yours,
your heart in mine,
sharing with the world
the bitter-sweet of your passion.

Kate, my dear,

I was so glad to have your quick response – and deeply moved, as so often, by those two very special poems. It amazes me that you could write them at a time when you are still wrestling with all the upheaval of this year, your physical weakness and lurking anxiety about whether you can manage at school in future. And I know you dread slipping back into the old pattern of trying to 'play things his way', but just as much that you may not be able to stop yourself giving vent at last to all the pain and resentment you hid away for so long, with the disastrous toll that took on you in the Spring. If you can write like this, though, I am quite certain that you will come through in the end, however long it may take to arrive at genuine forgiveness.

Now I understand why you didn't manage to share the poems on the day of the picnic! It was wonderful up there on the cliff-top, the two of us basking in the sun, but then Sister Nora suddenly appeared and swept us straight along to the retreat house for a cup of tea with the others. The three of them are surely the right people in the right place: each in her own way has such a gift of welcome and making everyone feel special: something that was always a feature of Celtic spirituality in the days of St Non and her son St David. Hospitality still is a characteristic of the monastic spirit today, of course, even amongst the hermit orders, with their stricter rules. It was lovely to see you so much at home with the sisters.

I remember from your student days that you were always strongly attracted to the Celtic 'atmosphere' and heritage in Pembrokeshire. You used to say that you knew who you were from within it, and that if you believed in reincarnation, you would know this was where you had come from! Also that part of your hunger for God was fed when you were 'immersed' in the natural world. (I know that's true. I realised at Freshwater West, when we witnessed that magnificent sunset over the rocky beach, that you were quite rapt by it, as if you were drinking it in, in great deep gulps.) The Celtic tradition did not make many of the sharp distinctions we make today. For them their experience of life was a single whole. Human life was completely woven in with the life of the elements and the animals. God breathed through them all.

You ask how you can possibly forgive your Head, and perhaps here some of the Celtic writings could be a help. They are so conscious that all of us are in the same boat, all belong together: before the face of God we are all so weak and small – and so much loved. In the wonderful book of Gaelic prayers called *The Sun Dances* there is a 'Death Blessing' with the lines

> *God, omit not this man from Thy covenant,*
> *and the many evils which he in the body*
>   *committed...*

> *Be this soul on Thine own arm, O Christ.*
> *Thou King of the City of Heaven;*
> *and since Thine it was, O Christ,*
>   *to buy the soul,*
> *at the time of the balancing of the beam,*
> *at the time of the bringing in the*
>   *judgement,*
> *be it now on Thy right hand.*

> *And be the holy Michael, king of angels ...*
> *coming to meet the soul,*
> *and leading it home*
> *to the heaven of the Son of God.*

That is a prayer for ourselves, for our enemies and for all who have hurt us. It might also help simply to say the Lord's Prayer as if you were standing alongside your Head, the words "Our Father" belonging to you both. Can you imagine yourself in his shoes, think about what may have led him to behave as he has towards you? Is it possible that he is caught up (just as you were) in some patterns from the past that have conditioned his reactions to you – in the same way that you, though you didn't realise it, were 'seeing' your early picture of your father in him, and reacting to that?

Perhaps that's all too difficult for now, but the seedling thought might grow a bit by itself, if it is set aside in a quiet corner of your heart, to be looked at gently from time to time with God, rather than being dismissed altogether. Meanwhile, we are so lucky, you and I, as we have often said, to have partners who will bear with us, give us the kind of space God gives, without making us feel we are neglecting them. It was great to see Pete and the boys come back tanned and happy from their trek along the Coastal Path, glad to be with you again and eager to start telling you the whole story. We are indeed surrounded by the 'cloud of witnesses' St Paul talks about; though half the time the witnesses do not have a clue that that is what they are for us – the 'saints' who don't know it!

I hope you enjoy meeting your old college friend next week. Isn't she the one you visited when she had a spell in hospital in London during your first year? After all this time there will certainly be plenty to catch up on. In the meantime I shall be spending two or three blissfully quiet days at the retreat house in Llannerchwen (Brecon Beacons) that I discovered last year. I wish I could take you with me to see it.

My love and prayers, as always, Kate,

Ailsa

My dear Kate

It isn't my turn to write, but I know I didn't get to tell you about Llannerchwen last year and I so much want to! My energy level is low today, though, so what I am sending is actually something I wrote down on my first visit. That's why the weather in it is so different from our present dull and cloudy spell. But nothing else has changed here. Second time around, I've fallen in love all over again with the place and its Creator. You must come and taste and see for yourself some day.

This is what is called a 'thin' place, here on the hillside at Llannerchwen, a place where earth feels very close to heaven. The sun is shining both outside and in, which does not always happen for me on retreat! Outside my window a large overhanging cherry-tree in full bloom is offering itself to me as a bouquet from the Bridegroom, saying, "I have brought you here to love you and for you to be aware of my loving." Beneath the tree there is a wooden gate, and beyond it a meadow that is home to rabbits, squirrels and pheasants – with the occasional sheep coming for a sleep-over. Beyond that again is the mountain range with the highest point of the Beacons, Pen–y-Fan, enfolded by mist in early morning, but growing more and more vivid as the day progresses.

The tree has become especially important, even as the mountain has become the Holy Mountain. One day when I sat under it eating lunch, a breeze shook its flowers, which fell like confetti showering down – a real wedding! I remembered reading that St Gregory of Nyssa, in his wonderful Homilies on the Song of Songs, says that the bride, no matter how much she has matured in the spiritual life, always seems to be just beginning the journey! That is how it has been for me here, a new beginning, through a gate into freedom. An awesome experience that is, for the most part, wordless. The stillness that is settled on the land here has seeped into my soul, in a silence broken only by birdsong. It made me doubt the value of words piled up on one another... Perhaps it is only when words are woven economically into poems that they have any deep-lasting value. The beauty to be en-countered here speaks by being. It reminds me so much of Gerard Manley Hopkins and his ideas about 'inscape':

As kingfishers catch fire, dragonflies draw
    flame;
As rounded over rim in roundy wells
Stones ring ...
Each mortal thing does one thing and the
    same:
Deals out that being indoors each one dwells;
Selves – goes itself; myself it speaks and spells;
Crying What I do is me: for that I came.'

Meeting the indwelling Christ of all things in the centre of myself, it is enough just to be here, without a mask, free from the judgement of others – to be part of it all, enfolded in love.

If this sounds romantic, Kate, you and I both know something of the reality behind the words: a glory so great, it's beyond our capacity to grasp it, except by the very edges! Part of me won't want to come home from here, and yet I know the glory is always there waiting for us, round the next corner, in the next person we encounter... if only our hearts and minds and eyes are ready to see it, the moment God chooses to lift the veil.

Much love and prayer, my dear,

Ailsa

Very dear Kate

This is a quick telegram in answer to your SOS!
I've only just got back home and found it.

No, your courage hasn't collapsed, and the hard-
won strength you've gained hasn't all drained
away to nothing. I know that is how it feels to
you, given the extraordinary outcome of meeting
up with your friend Maggie after so long. But
just hold on, Kate, and you will find, as you
have before, that the storm-tossed waves won't
swamp you – they will begin to look and behave
differently. Maggie may even turn out to have
done you an unwitting service.

This is how I see it, from what you have told me.
Once you'd discovered that Maggie had also gone
into teaching, later on, it was inevitable that you
would at least mention your current Head to her.
You weren't to know that she would recognise
his name from when she first started teaching
fourteen years ago; still less that she would go
straight on to describe an experience very like
your own, and in the same situation – he was
already a headmaster then. Evidently with time
she had completely come to terms with her

decision to leave the school at that point and begin again elsewhere: she talked about it only as a past episode, without lasting ill-effects beyond the financial hardship of the next few years. It wasn't until after your meeting with Maggie was over, you seem to be saying, that this vast rage arose in you on her behalf, for what the very same man had done to her life. And the most upsetting thing of all is that you feel you are back where you were before Easter, utterly out of control? – not this time beaten down and overcome by weakness, granted, but gripped by a vengeful anger, a kind of inner fury that refuses to subside.

Kate, this doesn't make you, in your words, an 'unacceptable' or hypocritical human being. Take it all into the silence of prayer, even if you feel like a bull in a china shop! God is still waiting for you there and doesn't say, "You can't come in until you behave better and are feeling repentant and generous and forgiving." His invitation is, "Come in, to my healing Presence. Acknowledge that though no conscious part of you may want to harbour such murderous anger, you are actually powerless to help yourself in the matter of how you feel. Put your trust in My promises: you already know them well. My ways may often be inscrutable to you, but I love you."

Be sure that I shall be holding you specially in prayer, and though they don't know it, I will be holding Maggie, and Derek, your Head, as well.

Much love to you, Kate. As best I can, I stand by you in your baptism of fire.

Ailsa

YOUR COMING

As the clamour dies

you come in the night

to my place of desolation

where life is laid bare,

with old wounds wide open

and love's loss complete.

Yet your coming changes everything

and peace falls like rain

soft on the parched soil of a scorched earth,

full-filling the underground caverns of emptiness,

as stillness settles silent

on a soul made ready to receive you.

"Lord, you are enough for me,"

falls almost unnoticed from between cracked lips

and you lift my eyelids

for me to see

the long life of your loving

that has led to this place:

God Himself

burning a pathway,

making room for His coming,

preparing space in the soul

through the very business of living.

THE STILL POINT

To the still point of the world

you bring me,

stripped of illusion,

need-naked before you:

to the foot of your cross

and the gentleness of God

where thought's wings fold in the heart

and future plans melt molten in the fire.

Vulnerable and alone,

hands empty before you,

gathered up in love's gaze

and embraced in your victory.

Dear Kate,

If I were one to say, "I told you so", you have given me lots of cause to do it! My dear godchild, dear friend, your letter brought me such happy news. I can hardly believe how quickly things have changed for you. Your poems speak volumes, and speak them so beautifully. It is a wonder to me that so much has happened in the short space of the summer holidays and all its family activities. Yet that only bears out what we talked about early in the year: even at the busiest times there are enough little pauses we can use to make contact with God, if we will. St Benedict says that prayer does not have to be long. The shortest turning to Him, as long as it is heartfelt, is better than all the lengthy praying that isn't.

You say the huge inner pressure has gone, you have swung back into place again like a compass needle, no longer cut off from others and from God. Restored to the living, breathing, inter-connecting relationships that are our life and sustenance, you can stand back from the anger you felt, not condemning it, though you regret it and the harm it could have done. It dawned upon you that the violence of it stemmed from your pent-up anger on your own behalf, rather than belonging to Maggie's story. And that has helped even further, because you feel you have drawn strength from the whole episode, as if energy always locked up in you before was liberated, to be a resource for the future that you can put to good and creative use. (It's already there, in fact, in your poems, which have the power to touch many lives, if you are willing to let people share them.) But in any case what you have gained is another precious insight which, as you say, puts the whole world in a different light, simultaneously anchoring us and setting us free. We will go through many troughs and highs again, but with each one we will know better how to recognise the dangers in advance and avoid them, or how to hold on when the going gets rough.

Your second poem reminds me of words St Augustine puts into the mouth of the dying thief, asked how he knew who Jesus was – had he read the Scriptures? "No, I haven't. But Jesus looked at me, and in that look I understood everything." You say my letters have helped you start to believe that God is in every situation and that then everything looks less black. Going further, daring to look into the dark void that seems to be meaningless (though St John of the Cross would call it love!) you found something shifted.

You recognised Christ was there, and had been all along, and with that the torment and the sense of isolation melted away and the prayer of abandonment was yours again, at a deeper level than before.

I am so glad your panic has been dissipated and you are restored to yourself, calm and able to cope again. It is how the prodigal son must have felt when the nightmare was over and he returned to find his father waiting with no reproach for him, only with heartfelt welcome. There is a poem by someone that ends with an amazed and joyous cry, "Look, we have come home!" And we do, to God and to our innermost selves: both, strangely, to be found occupying the same space within us.

Now I must stop – but not before saying how glad I was to hear that the doctor thinks there may be no radical harm to your spine, it may well heal fully if you continue to go carefully for the next two or three months. How marvellous that young Harry is learning to cook, to help you out next term! The blessings come thick and fast this year, don't they, despite the testing times? It's quite something when your son will volunteer to take time out from his computer games!

So much love to you, and my prayers, as always.

Ailsa

My dear Kate,

You wrote about your gladness at picking up again with Maggie and finding you had even more in common now than in your student days. Lately I've been musing a lot on the networks of fellowship beyond the family, the various groups and individuals with whom we are bound up by our life-situation and our deliberate choices, from whom we often draw vital support. So many share, as do you and I, the sense of God calling us to live out our discipleship as fully and deeply as we can. You have found that, I know, in your contemplative prayer group. Of course this is the call to all Christians. But right now there appears to be a movement of the Holy Spirit sweeping like a wave through the hearts and minds of many, encouraging them to trust their intuition that it isn't necessary to adopt some special way of life in order to follow Christ without reserve. It can be done not in spite of, but through the ordinary wage-earning and domestic activities of our world. The 'one thing necessary' isn't a special lifestyle like that of monks, nuns and priests. It is rather that for no one should anything matter more than God, and that we should all do our utmost to bring every aspect of our lives into line with that.

We know nothing God has made is by its nature incapable of revealing Him to us. What matters is whether we use the gifts of God to His glory or not. According to St Irenaeus, the glory of God is "the human being who is fully alive", matured in charity and wisdom. While those qualities often shine out in people living a cloistered life, they can equally be won "without leaving your day job", as Brother Benet Tredten said to the Oblates* of Blue Cloud Abbey. They come to us by way of constant sacrificial love – plenty of scope for that in our everyday lives! It's true that some few are still called, in the time-honoured way, to desert or cloister as 'their' place for becoming more fully human and knowing God more deeply. But many others today, just as hungry and thirsty for total commitment to God, need to understand that vocation is not about choosing one thing over another, religious life over marriage, for example. There is one vocation

---

* Oblates are individuals linked with a religious house who adopt a certain rule of life associated with it, but normally live that out in their ordinary lives, outside any monastery or convent.

for everyone, and that is the fullest, deepest possible relationship with God. And we live this out – you know what I'm going to say! – in myriad ways, according to our circumstances.

I suppose this comes to mind every time the Spirit grants us a fresh gleam of insight into God and the nature of His love. The result is always greater freedom for us to give of ourselves. It's as if we are each given a trail of special moments, like a custom-made string of lights, winding through the days and years of our individual lives. With every new lamp that comes into view, He is showing us the way ahead, step by step, enabling us to walk it, and bringing us home to Himself.

Although words are always so inadequate, I'm sending you some lines that came to me when I was at Llannerchwen, written out of that centre of stillness which always awaits us. I pray that the sense of the holy place – the poustinia within – will still be there for you, like the sea and the sky in the background of a painting, while you attend to all the foreground mental bustle of preparing this term's lesson plans – and even when you step into the classroom again in ten days' time. (By the way, I might be away from home just then, as I have to go into hospital for a day or two – only some minor tests. But I imagine you'll be far too busy to report back straight away in any case, so I shall have an excellent opportunity to practise the virtue of patience!)

Much love – keep up your courage!

Ailsa

ON THE HILLSIDE

Alone on the hillside...

The stillness of your presence

pierces

the blindness of this run-rabbit day,

and as the sun sets in glory on the distant horizon

creation hangs

hushed

in the silence of eternity.

Drawn here by love to this deep heart of mystery,

hardly daring to breathe,

I give you my hand;

a small child, enraptured by the smile of her
    father,

I give you my "Yes –

let it be your way..."

No plans of my own in this land of unknowing,

only willing to go where love wishes to lead.

DANCE

How patient you have been

teaching me to dance!

Fluid now, though, and free,

partners in love facing each other,

you lead,

I follow,

first this way, then that,

through sunlight and darkness,

from moment to moment

close to your heartbeat

and in tune with your step,

towards the wounds of the World

or the beauty of her being;

happy at last

in this stillness that is dancing.

Dearest Kate,

I'm feeling much better, thank you – not least for having your phone call and your letter. In both you sounded so strong and relaxed. I do know what you mean when you speak of the "two-way feeling". You have come back to the same place, the school where you've taught for three years, and found it mercifully new and different – not the same place of anxiety and oppression that it was for so long. Yet it also feels like home, as if you had been for a long time estranged from your true self, and have now returned to the familiar 'you', the one that has the potential to forgive and will not shrink back into your shell again.

I'm sure you are right not to be counting chickens, though! As you say, there is far more to it than merely framing the words "I forgive you", aloud or silently. I think of the process of forgiveness as like the layers of an onion. Though we can peel it right down to the final layer, that can't be removed except by the pure gift of God; which is something we can only receive. That last layer is surely what the Redemptorist priest Jim McManus calls being reconciled with the one at whose hands we have been hurt. "Often people are held back," he says, "by believing that if they are truly to forgive someone, they must be reconciled to them." This, he says, is a mistake. It may be a long time before reconciliation comes, however strong our trust in God's healing power. Meanwhile there is much we can and should do that is indispensable to the work of forgiving.

Another wise priest said that we must learn to co-operate with God in forgiving ourselves. When, out of deep pain and hurt, resentment keeps showing its ugly face, we don't want to feel it. We may sometimes think we have shed it all, but then it suddenly pops up again from inside, like an unstoppable jack-in-the-box weed. We mustn't be disheartened; the only recourse is on every occasion simply to show the resentment the door, not be tempted to keep hold of it. With God's help there will come a day when we really are free to choose just that and it happens once and for all. Or if necessary we must summon all our courage and 'step over' our wounds – even to putting distance between ourselves and the one who caused them (as Maggie did), if that is open to us. In your case you came to see that your vulnerability stems from much earlier times with your father, so moving away from here might not have done very much to solve the problem. Failing all else, if we freely admit that we have no power of ourselves to take this 'step across', it is our privilege to follow Jesus' example and ask God to do it for us: "Father forgive them – they don't know what they are doing."

Being enabled to forgive is, for the person hurt, a true gift of healing, a liberation and a gateway to freedom. But because, from our changed viewpoint, we behave differently with those we have forgiven, things mysteriously change for the better in them and their lives too – even if neither of us quite understands how or why. Isn't this the best part of all about forgiveness, the unexpected flowering of our struggles; like the Cross, described by early poets as the dead tree which has wondrously come through pain and death into full bloom?

Thank you for reminding me of your earlier poem, Kate. No, "It isn't easy being made, submitting to the melting down and hammering into shape, feeling only the pain without knowing the beauty" – which is yet to come. And yes, "Only stillness helps" during that stage, "relaxing … into the sure hands of the Craftsman", trusting that His work will prove fit for His chosen purpose and become a chalice to hold "the wine of His presence" offered to all. I'm not surprised that you've found new levels of meaning in your own words now. It is such an unimaginable privilege to work with and for Him in this way.

And the new poem you sent, 'Dance', not only describes the next stage of your journey; it has set my pen to work too. Walking beside you seems to have given me back a fluency I thought had left me long ago! Thank you, Kate, for this and for much else. I'm so glad to look on, as you become more and more your lovely self – can't wait to see what the next moves will be in the glorious dance. How lucky you are in Pete and Oliver and Harry, too. They may not know much about the steps, but they don't need to: they are always there, keeping in time and part of the flow. Give them my love. It will be great to see you all at half-term, if we can manage to call by for tea on our journey northwards. We'll be in touch before then.

Always with prayer and pride in you,

Your loving Ailsa

He said to me:

"To the place where I will take you

bring nothing except yourself.

Bring no gifts for me

- of work or of the spirit -

except yourself.

And from this place

you will return with no trophies

- either of deed or experience –

neither will you be able to tell where you've been;

and only those who have been there themselves
        will understand.

But I shall give you my peace to go with you,

and my joy for you to share with others.

One night of deepest dark,

my heart with flame of ardent love afire,

- ah! grace most blest and rare! -

I ventured forth, no witness as I went,

leaving my house behind me, now all stilled.

On that graced night I left

in secret, keeping far from others' sight

nor seeing any thing myself, in that deep dark,

and lacking guide or light

save that alone which in my heart was lit:

Its glowing led me on

more surely than the light of noonday clear,

to where One waited near

whose presence I knew well -

the place so hid, no other would come there.

St John of the Cross
'Dark Night' stanzas 1,3 and 4
(trans., Benedicta)